FIRESIDE CHATS

FRANKLIN DELANO ROOSEVELT

FIRESIDE CHATS

penguin books

PENGUIN BOOKS
Published by the Penguin Group
Penguin Books USA Inc., 375 Hudson Street,
New York, New York 10014, U.S.A.
Penguin Books Ltd, 27 Wrights Lane,
London W8 5TZ, England
Penguin Books Australia Ltd, Ringwood,
Victoria, Australia
Penguin Books Canada Ltd, 10 Alcorn Avenue,
Toronto, Ontario, Canada M4V 3B2
Penguin Books (N.Z.) Ltd, 182–190 Wairau Road,
Auckland 10, New Zealand

Penguin Books Ltd, Registered Offices:
Harmondsworth, Middlesex, England

Published in Penguin Books 1995

ISBN 0 14 60.0100 1

Printed in the United States of America

These eight Fireside Chats were selected from the thirty-one talks over the radio President Roosevelt gave to the nation. They present his leadership on the two most significant events of his presidency, the establishment of the New Deal during the economic crisis of the Great Depression and his command of the nation during the Second World War.

The New Deal

MARCH 12, 1933

My friends, I want to talk for a few minutes with the people of the United States about banking—to talk with the comparatively few who understand the mechanics of banking, but more particularly with the overwhelming majority of you who use banks for the making of deposits and the drawing of checks. I want to tell you what has been done in the last few days, and why it was done, and what the next steps are going to be. I recognize that the many proclamations from the state capitals and from Washington, the legislation, the Treasury regulations and so forth, couched for the most part in banking and legal terms, ought to be explained for the benefit of the average citizen. I owe this in particular because of the fortitude and the good temper with which everybody has accepted the inconvenience and the hardships of the banking holiday. And I know that when you understand what we in Washington have been about I shall continue to have your cooperation as fully as I have had your sympathy and your help during the past week.

First of all, let me state the simple fact that when you deposit money in a bank the bank does not put the money into a safe deposit vault. It invests your money in many different forms of credit—in bonds, in commercial paper, in mortgages, and in many other kinds of loans. In other words, the bank puts your money to work to keep the wheels of industry and of agriculture turning round. A comparatively small part of the money that you put into the bank is kept in currency—an amount which in normal times is wholly sufficient to cover the cash needs of the average citizen. In other words, the total amount of all the currency in the country is only a comparatively small proportion of the total deposits in all the banks of the country.

What, then, happened during the last few days of February and the first few days of March? Because of undermined confidence on the part of the public, there was a general rush by a large portion of our population to turn bank deposits into currency or gold—a rush so great that the soundest banks couldn't get enough currency to meet the demand. The reason for this was that on the spur of the moment it was, of course, impossible to sell perfectly sound assets of a bank and convert them into cash except at panic prices far below their real value.

By the afternoon of March 3, a week ago last Friday, scarcely a bank in the country was open to do business. Proclamations closing them in whole or in part had been issued by the governors in almost all of the states.

It was then that I issued the proclamation providing for
2   the national bank holiday, and this was the first step in the

government's reconstruction of our financial and economic fabric.

The second step, last Thursday, was the legislation promptly and patriotically passed by the Congress confirming my proclamation and broadening my powers so that it became possible in view of the requirement of time to extend the holiday and lift the ban of that holiday gradually in the days to come. This law also gave authority to develop a program of rehabilitation of our banking facilities, and I want to tell our citizens in every part of the nation that the national Congress—Republicans and Democrats alike—showed by this action a devotion to public welfare and a realization of the emergency and the necessity for speed that it is difficult to match in all our history.

The third stage has been the series of regulations permitting the banks to continue their functions to take care of the distribution of food and household necessities and the payment of payrolls.

This bank holiday, while resulting in many cases in great inconvenience, is affording us the opportunity to supply the currency necessary to meet the situation. Remember that no sound bank is a dollar worse off than it was when it closed its doors last week. Neither is any bank which may turn out not to be in a position for immediate opening. The new law allows the twelve federal reserve banks to issue additional currency on good assets and thus banks that reopen will be able to meet every legitimate call. The new currency is being 3 sent out by the Bureau of Engraving and Printing in large volume to every part of the country. It is sound currency because it is backed by actual, good assets.

Another question that you will ask is this: why are all the banks not to be reopened at the same time? The answer is simple, and I know you will understand it. Your government does not intend that the history of the past few years shall be repeated. We do not want and will not have another epidemic of bank failures.

As a result, we start tomorrow, Monday, with the opening of banks in the twelve federal reserve bank cities—those banks which on first examination by the Treasury have already been found to be all right. That will be followed on Tuesday by the resumption of all other functions by banks already found to be sound in cities where there are recognized clearing houses. That means about 250 cities of the United States. In other words, we are moving as fast as the mechanics of the situation will allow us.

On Wednesday and succeeding days banks in smaller places all through the country will resume business, subject, of course, to the government's physical ability to complete its survey. It is necessary that the reopening of banks be extended over a period in order to permit the banks to make applications for the necessary loans, to obtain currency needed to meet their requirements, and to enable the government to make commonsense checkups.

4   Please let me make it clear to you that if your bank does

not open the first day, you are by no means justified in believing that it will not open. A bank that opens on one of the subsequent days is in exactly the same status as the bank that opens tomorrow.

I know that many people are worrying about state banks that are not members of the Federal Reserve System. There is no occasion for that worry. These banks can and will receive assistance from member banks and from the Reconstruction Finance Corporation and of course they are under the immediate control of the state banking authorities. These state banks are following the same course as the national banks except that they get their licenses to resume business from the state authorities, and these authorities have been asked by the secretary of the treasury to permit their good banks to open up on the same schedule as the national banks. And so I am confident that the state banking departments will be as careful as the national government in the policy relating to the opening of banks and will follow the same broad theory.

It is possible that when the banks resume a very few people who have not recovered from their fear may again begin withdrawals. Let me make it clear to you that the banks will take care of all needs except of course the hysterical demands of hoarders—and it is my belief that hoarding during the past week has become an exceedingly unfashionable pastime in every part of our nation. It needs no prophet to tell you that when the people find that they can get their money— 5 that they can get it when they want it for all legitimate purposes—the phantom of fear will soon be laid. People will again be glad to have their money where it will be safely taken care of and where they can use it conveniently at any time. I can assure you, my friends, that it is safer to keep your money in a reopened bank than it is to keep it under the mattress.

The success of our whole national program depends, of course, on the cooperation of the public—on its intelligent support and its use of a reliable system.

Remember that the essential accomplishment of the new legislation is that it makes it possible for banks more readily to convert their assets into cash than was the case before. More liberal provision has been made for banks to borrow on these assets at the reserve banks and more liberal provision has also been made for issuing currency on the security of these good assets. This currency is not fiat currency. It is issued only on adequate security, and every good bank has an abundance of such security.

One more point before I close. There will be, of course, some banks unable to reopen without being reorganized. The new law allows the government to assist in making these reorganizations quickly and effectively and even allows the government to subscribe to at least a part of any new capital that may be required.

6   I hope you can see, my friends, from this essential recital

of what your government is doing that there is nothing complex, nothing radical, in the process.

We had a bad banking situation. Some of our bankers had shown themselves either incompetent or dishonest in their handling of the people's funds. They had used the money entrusted to them in speculations and unwise loans. This was, of course, not true in the vast majority of our banks, but it was true in enough of them to shock the people of the United States for a time into a sense of insecurity and to put them into a frame of mind where they did not differentiate, but seemed to assume that the acts of a comparative few had tainted them all. And so it became the government's job to straighten out this situation and to do it as quickly as possible. And that job is being performed.

I do not promise you that every bank will be reopened or that individual losses will not be suffered, but there will be no losses that possibly could be avoided; and there would have been more and greater losses had we continued to drift. I can even promise you salvation for some at least of the sorely pressed banks. We shall be engaged not merely in reopening sound banks but in the creation of more sound banks through reorganization.

It has been wonderful to me to catch the note of confidence from all over the country. I can never be sufficiently grateful to the people for the loyal support that they have given me in their acceptance of the judgment that has dic- 7 tated our course, even though all our processes may not have seemed clear to them.

After all, there is an element in the readjustment of our financial system more important than currency, more important than gold, and that is the confidence of the people themselves. Confidence and courage are the essentials of success in carrying out our plan. You people must have faith; you must not be stampeded by rumors or guesses. Let us unite in banishing fear. We have provided the machinery to restore our financial system; and it is up to you to support and make it work.

It is your problem, my friends, your problem no less than it is mine. Together we cannot fail.

May 7, 1933

On a Sunday night a week after my inauguration I used the radio to tell you about the banking crisis and about the measures we were taking to meet it. In that way I tried to make clear to the country various facts that might otherwise have been misunderstood and in general to provide a means of understanding which I believe did much to restore confidence.

Tonight, eight weeks later, I come for the second time to
give you my report, in the same spirit and by the same

means, to tell you about what we have been doing and what we are planning to do.

Two months ago as you know we were facing serious problems. The country was dying by inches. It was dying because trade and commerce had declined to dangerously low levels; prices for basic commodities were such as to destroy the value of the assets of national institutions such as banks, and savings banks, and insurance companies, and others. These institutions, because of their great needs, were foreclosing mortgages, they were calling loans, and they were refusing credit. Thus there was actually in process of destruction the property of millions of people who had borrowed money on that property in terms of dollars which had had an entirely different value from the level of March 1933. That situation in that crisis did not call for any complicated consideration of economic panaceas or fancy plans. We were faced by a condition and not a theory

There were just two alternatives at that time: The first was to allow the foreclosures to continue, credit to be withheld, money to go into hiding, thus forcing liquidation and bankruptcy of banks and railroads and insurance companies and a recapitalizing of all business and all property on a lower level. That alternative meant a continuation of what is loosely called "deflation," the net result of which would have been extraordinary hardships on all property owners and all bank depositors, and incidentally, extraordinary hardships on all persons working for wages through an increase in unemployment and a further reduction of the wage scale.

It is easy to see that the result of that course would have not only economic effects of a very serious nature, but social results also that might bring incalculable harm. Even before I was inaugurated I came to the conclusion that such a policy was too much to ask the American people to bear. It involved not only a further loss of homes and farms and savings and wages, but also a loss of spiritual values—the loss of that sense of security for the present and the future that is so necessary to the peace and contentment of the individual and of his family. When you destroy those things you find it difficult to establish confidence of any sort in the future. And it is clear that mere appeals coming out of Washington for more confidence and the mere lending of more money to shaky institutions could not stop that downward course. A prompt program applied as quickly as possible seemed to me not only justified but imperative to our national security. The Congress, and when I say the Congress I mean the members of both political parties, fully understood this and gave me generous and intelligent support. The members of the Congress realized that the methods of normal times had to be replaced in the emergency by measures that were suited to the serious and pressing requirements of the moment. There was no actual surrender of power. Congress still retains its constitutional authority to legislate and to appropriate, and no one has the slightest desire to change the balance of these powers.

The function of Congress is to decide what has to be done and to select the appropriate agency to carry out its will. That policy it has strictly adhered to. The only thing that has been happening has been to designate the president of the United States as the agency to carry out certain of the purposes of the Congress. This was constitutional and is constitutional, and it is in keeping with the past American tradition.

The legislation that has been passed or is in the process of enactment can properly be considered as part of a well-grounded, well-rounded plan.

First, we are giving opportunity of employment to a quarter of a million of the unemployed, especially the young men who have dependents, to let them go into forestry and flood-prevention work. That is a big task because it means feeding and clothing and caring for nearly twice as many men as we have in the regular Army itself. And in creating this Civilian Conservation Corps we are killing two birds with one stone. We are clearly enhancing the value of our natural resources, and at the same time we are relieving an appreciable amount of actual distress. This great group of men, young men, have entered upon their work on a purely voluntary basis; no military training is involved and we are conserving not only our natural resources, but also our human resources. One of the great values to this work is the fact that it is direct and requires the intervention of very little machinery.

Secondly, I have requested the Congress and have secured

action upon a proposal to put the great properties owned by our government at Muscle Shoals to work after long years of wasteful inaction, and with this goes hand-in-hand a broad plan for the permanent improvement of the vast area included in the whole of the Tennessee Valley. It will add to the comfort and to the happiness of hundreds of thousands of people and the incident benefits will reach the entire nation.

Next, the Congress is about to pass legislation that will greatly ease the mortgage distress among the farmers and among the home-owners of the nation, by providing for the easing of the burden of debt that now bears so heavily upon millions of our people.

Our next step in seeking immediate relief is a grant of half a billion dollars to help the states and the counties and the municipalities in their duty to care for those who at this time need direct and immediate relief.

In addition to all this, the Congress also passed legislation as you know authorizing the sale of beer in such states as desired it. That has already resulted in considerable reemployment, and incidentally it has provided for the federal government and for the states a much-needed tax revenue.

Now as to the future.

We are planning within a few days to ask the Congress for legislation to enable the government to undertake public works, thus stimulating directly and indirectly the employment of many others in well-considered projects.

Further legislation has been taken up which goes much more fundamentally into our economic problems. The Farm Relief Bill seeks by the use of several methods, alone or together, to bring about an increased return to farmers for their major farm products, seeking at the same time to prevent in the days to come disastrous overproduction, the kind of overproduction that so often in the past has kept farm commodity prices far below a reasonable return. This measure provides wide powers for emergencies and the extent of its use will depend entirely upon what the future has in store.

Well-considered and conservative measures will likewise be proposed, within a few days, that will attempt to give to the industrial workers of the country a more fair wage return, to prevent cutthroat competition, to prevent unduly long hours for labor, and at the same time to encourage each industry to prevent overproduction.

One of our bills falls into the same class, the Railroad Bill. It seeks to provide and make certain a definite planning by the railroads themselves, with the assistance of the government, in order to eliminate the duplication and the waste that now results in railroad receiverships and in continuing operating deficits.

I feel very certain that the people of this country understand and approve the broad purposes behind these new governmental policies relating to agriculture and industry and transportation. We found ourselves faced with more agricultural products than we could possibly consume ourselves and with surpluses which other nations did not have the cash to buy from us except at prices ruinously low. We found our factories able to turn out more goods than we could possibly consume, and at the same time we have been faced with a falling export demand. We have found ourselves with more facilities to transport goods and crops than there were goods and crops to be transported. All of this has been caused in large part by a complete lack of planning and a complete failure to understand the danger signals that have been flying ever since the close of the World War. The people of this country have been erroneously encouraged to believe that they could keep on increasing the output of farm and of factory indefinitely and that some magician would find ways and means for that increased output to be consumed with reasonable profit to the producer.

But today we have reason to believe that things are a little better than they were two months ago. Industry has picked up, railroads are carrying more freight, farm prices are better. But I am not going to indulge in issuing proclamations of overenthusiastic assurance. We cannot ballyhoo ourselves back to prosperity and I am going to be honest at all times with the people of the country. I do not want the people of this country to take the foolish course of letting this improvement come back on another speculative wave. I do not want the people to believe that because of unjustified optimism we 14 can resume the ruinous practice of increasing our crop output and our factory output in the hope that a kind Providence will find buyers at high prices. Such a course may bring us immediate and false prosperity but it will be the kind of prosperity that will lead us into another tailspin.

It is wholly wrong to call the measures that we have taken government control of farming or government control of industry, or a government control of transportation. It is rather a partnership—a partnership between government and farming, a partnership between government and industry, and a partnership between government and transportation. Not a partnership in profits, because the profits will still go to the private citizen, but rather a partnership in planning, and a partnership to see that the plans are carried out.

Let me illustrate with an example. Take for instance the cotton-goods industry. It is probably true that 90 percent of the cotton manufacturers of this country would agree tomorrow to eliminate starvation wages, would agree to stop long hours of employment, would agree to stop child labor, would agree to prevent an overproduction that would result in unsalable surpluses. But, my friends, what good is such an agreement of the 90 percent if the other 10 percent of the cotton manufacturers pay starvation wages and require long hours and employ children in their mills and turn out burdensome surpluses? The unfair 10 percent could produce goods so cheaply that the fair 90 percent would be compelled to meet the unfair conditions. And that is where government comes in. Government ought to have the right and will have 15 the right, after surveying and planning for an industry, to prevent, with the assistance of the overwhelming majority of that industry, all unfair practices and to enforce that agreement by the authority of government. The so-called antitrust laws were intended to prevent the creation of monopolies and to forbid unreasonable profits to those monopolies. That purpose of the antitrust laws must be continued, but those laws were never intended to encourage the kind of unfair competition that results in long hours and starvation wages and overproduction.

And, my friends, the same principle that is illustrated by that example applies to farm products and to transportation and to every other field of organized private industry.

We are working towards a definite goal, a goal that seeks to prevent the return of conditions which came very close to destroying what we alive call modern civilization. The actual accomplishment of our purposes cannot be attained in a day. Our policies are wholly within the purposes for which our American constitutional government was established 150 years ago.

I know that the people of this country will understand this and that they will also understand the spirit in which we are undertaking that policy. I do not deny that we may make some mistakes of procedure as we carry out this policy. I have no expectation of making a hit every time I come to bat. What I seek is the highest possible batting average, not only for myself but for the team. Theodore Roosevelt once said to me, "If I can be right 75 percent of the time, I shall come up to the fullest measure of my hopes."

Much has been said of late about federal finances and inflation, about the gold standard, and francs and pounds and so forth. I should like to make the facts very simple and to make my policy very clear. In the first place, government credit and government currency are really one and the same thing. Behind government bonds there is only a promise to pay. Behind government currency we have, in addition to the promise to pay, a reserve of gold and a small reserve of silver, neither of them anything like the total amount of the currency. And in this connection it is worthwhile remembering that in the past the government has agreed to redeem nearly 30 billions of its debts and its currency in gold, and private corporations and individuals in this country have agreed to redeem another 60 or 70 billions of securities and mortgages in gold. The government and the private corporations and individuals were making these agreements when they knew full well that all of the gold in the United States amounted to only between 3 and 4 billion and that all of the gold in all of the world amounted to only about 11 billion.

If the holders of these promises to pay were all of them to start in to demand gold the firstcomers would get gold for a few days or a few hours and those firstcomers who would get the gold would amount to about one twenty-fifth of all of the holders of the securities and the currency. The other twenty-four people out of twenty-five, who did not happen to be at the top of the line, would be politely told that there was no more gold left. And so we have decided in Washington to treat all twenty-five people in the same way in the interest of justice and in the exercise of the constitutional powers of this government. We placed everyone on the same basis in order that the general good may be preserved.

Nevertheless, gold, and to a partial extent silver also, are perfectly good bases for currency, and that is why I decided not to let any of the gold now in the country go out of it.

A series of conditions arose three weeks ago which very readily might have meant, first, a drain on our gold by foreign countries, and secondly, as a result of that drain, a flight of American capital itself, in the form of gold, out of our country. And it is not exaggerating the possibility to tell you that such an occurrence might well have taken from us the major part of our gold reserve and might well have resulted in such a further weakening of our government and private credit as to bring on actual panic conditions and the complete stoppage of the wheels of industry.

The administration has the definite objective of raising commodity prices to such an extent that those who have borrowed money will, on the average, be able to repay that money in the same kind of dollar which they borrowed. We do not seek to let them get such a cheap dollar that in effect they will be able to pay a great deal less back than they borrowed. In other words, we seek to correct a wrong and not to create another wrong in the opposite direction. That is why powers are being given to the administration to provide, if necessary, for an enlargement of credit, in order to correct the existing wrong. These powers will be used when, as, and if it may be necessary to accomplish the purpose.

Hand in hand with the domestic situation which, of course, is our first concern, is the world situation, and I want to emphasize to you that the domestic situation is inevitably and deeply tied in with the conditions in all of the other nations of the world. In other words, we can get, in all probability, some measure of return of prosperity in the United States, but it will not be permanent unless we can get a return to prosperity all over the world.

In the conferences that we have held and are holding with the leaders of other nations, we are seeking four great objectives: first, a general reduction of armaments and through this the removal of the fear of invasion and of armed attack, and, at the same time, a reduction in armament costs in order to help in the balancing of government budgets and in the reduction of taxation; secondly, a cutting down of the trade barriers, in order to restart the flow of exchange of crops and goods between nations; third, we seek the setting up of a stabilization of currencies, in order that trade and commerce can make contracts ahead; and fourth, we seek the reestablishment of friendly relations and greater confidence between all nations.

Our foreign visitors these past three weeks have responded to these purposes in a very helpful way. All of the nations have suffered alike in this great depression. They have all reached the conclusion that each can best be helped by the common action of all. And it is in this spirit that our visitors have met with us and discussed our common problems. The great international conference of this summer that lies before us must succeed. The future of the world demands it, and we have each of us pledged ourselves to the best joint efforts to that end.

To you, the people of this country, all of us in Washington, the members of the Congress and the members of this administration, owe a profound debt of gratitude. Throughout the depression you have been patient. You have granted us wide powers; you have encouraged us with a widespread approval of our purposes. Every ounce of strength, every resource at our command, we have devoted and we are devoting to the end of justifying your confidence. We are encouraged to believe that a wise and sensible beginning has been made. In the present spirit of mutual confidence, in the present spirit of mutual encouragement we go forward.

And in conclusion, my friends, may I express to the National Broadcasting Company and to the Columbia Broadcasting System my thanks for the facilities which they have made available to me tonight.

July 24, 1933

After the adjournment of the historical special session of the Congress five weeks ago I purposely refrained from addressing you for two very good reasons.

First, I think that we all wanted the opportunity of a little quiet thought to examine and assimilate in a mental picture the crowding events of the hundred days which had been devoted to the starting of the wheels of the New Deal.

Secondly, I wanted a few weeks in which to set up the new administrative organization and to see the first fruits of our careful planning.

I think it will interest you if I set forth the fundamentals of this planning for national recovery; and this I am very certain will make it abundantly clear to you that all of the proposals and all of the legislation since the fourth day of March have not been just a collection of haphazard schemes but rather the orderly component parts of a connected and logical whole.

Long before inauguration day I became convinced that individual effort and local effort and even disjointed federal effort had failed and of necessity would fail and, therefore, that a rounded leadership by the federal government had become a necessity both of theory and of fact. Such leadership, however, had its beginning in preserving and strengthening the credit of the United States government, because without that no leadership was a possibility. For years the government had not lived within its income. The immediate task was to bring our regular expenses within our revenues. That has been done.

It may seem inconsistent for a government to cut down its regular expenses and at the same time to borrow and to spend billions for an emergency. But it is not inconsistent because a large portion of the emergency money has been paid out in the form of sound loans which will be repaid to the Treasury over a period of years; and to cover the rest of the emergency money we have imposed taxes to pay the interest and the installments on that part of the debt.

So you will see that we have kept our credit good. We have built a granite foundation in a period of confusion. That foundation of the federal credit stands there broad and sure. It is the base of the whole recovery plan.

Then came the part of the problem that concerned the credit of the individual citizens themselves. You and I know of the banking crisis and of the great danger of the savings of our people. On March 6 every national bank was closed. One month later 90 percent of the deposits in the national banks had been made available to the depositors. Today only about 5 percent of the deposits in national banks are still tied

up. The condition relating to state banks, while not quite so good on a percentage basis, is showing a steady reduction in the total of frozen deposits—a result much better than we had expected three months ago.

The problem of the credit of the individual was made more difficult because of another fact. The dollar was a different dollar from the one with which the average debt had been incurred. For this reason large numbers of people were actually losing possession of and title of their farms and homes. All of you know the financial steps which have been taken to correct this inequality. In addition the Home Loan Act, the Farm Loan Act, and the bankruptcy act were passed.

It was a vital necessity to restore purchasing power by reducing the debt and interest charges upon our people, but while we were helping people to save their credit it was at the same time absolutely essential to do something about the physical needs of hundreds of thousands who were in dire straits at that very moment. Municipal and state aid were being stretched to the limit. We appropriated half a billion dollars to supplement their efforts and in addition, as you know, we have put 300,000 young men into practical and useful work in our forests and to prevent flood and soil erosion. The wages they earn are going in greater part to the support of the nearly 1 million people who constitute their families.

In this same classification we can properly place the great public works program running to a total of over $3 billion—to be used for highways and ships and flood preven- 23 tion and inland navigation and thousands of self-sustaining state and municipal improvements. Two points should be made clear in the allotting and administration of these projects—first, we are using the utmost care to choose labor creating quick-acting, useful projects, avoiding the smell of the pork barrel; and secondly, we are hoping that at least half of the money will come back to the government from projects which will pay for themselves over a period of years.

Thus far I have spoken primarily of the foundation stones—the measures that were necessary to reestablish credit and to head people in the opposite direction by preventing distress and providing as much work as possible through governmental agencies. Now I come to the links which will build us a more lasting prosperity. I have said that we cannot attain that in a nation half-boom and half-broke. If all of our people have work and fair wages and fair profits, they can buy the products of their neighbors and business is good. But if you take away the wages and the profits of half of them, business is only half as good. It doesn't help much if the fortunate half is very prosperous—the best way is for everybody to be reasonably prosperous.

For many years the two great barriers to a normal prosperity have been low farm prices and the creeping paralysis of unemployment. These factors have cut the purchasing power of the country in half. I promised action. Congress did its part when it passed the farm and the industrial recovery acts.

Today we are putting these two acts to work and they will work if people understand their plain objectives.

First, the farm act: It is based on the fact that the purchasing power of nearly half our population depends on adequate prices for farm products. We have been producing more of some crops than we consume or can sell in a depressed world market. The cure is not to produce so much. Without our help the farmers cannot get together and cut production, and the farm bill gives them a method of bringing their production down to a reasonable level and of obtaining reasonable prices for their crops. I have clearly stated that this method is in a sense experimental, but so far as we have gone we have reason to believe that it will produce good results.

It is obvious that if we can greatly increase the purchasing power of the tens of millions of our people who make a living from farming and the distribution of farm crops, we will greatly increase the consumption of those goods which are turned out by industry.

That brings me to the final step: bringing back industry along sound lines.

Last autumn, on several occasions, I expressed my faith that we can make possible by democratic self-discipline in industry general increases in wages and shortening of hours sufficient to enable industry to pay its own workers enough to let those workers buy and use the things that their labor produces. This can be done only if we permit and encourage 25 cooperative action in industry because it is obvious that without united action a few selfish men in each competitive group will pay starvation wages and insist on long hours of work. Others in that group must either follow suit or close up shop. We have seen the result of action of that kind in the continuing descent into the economic hell of the past four years.

There is a clear way to reverse that process: If all employers in each competitive group agree to pay their workers the same wages—reasonable wages—and require the same hours—reasonable hours—then higher wages and shorter hours will hurt no employer. Moreover, such action is better for the employer than unemployment and low wages, because it makes more buyers for his product. That is the simple idea which is the very heart of the Industrial Recovery Act.

On the basis of this simple principle of everybody doing things together, we are starting out on this nationwide attack on unemployment. It will succeed if our people understand it—in the big industries, in the little shops, in the great cities and in the small villages. There is nothing complicated about it and there is nothing particularly new in the principle. It goes back to the basic idea of society and of the nation itself that people acting in a group can accomplish things which no individual acting alone could even hope to bring about.

Here is an example. In the cotton textile code and in other agreements already signed, child labor has been abolished.

That makes me personally happier than any other one thing

with which I have been connected since I came to Washington. In the textile industry—an industry which came to me spontaneously and with a splendid cooperation as soon as the Recovery Act was signed—child labor was an old evil. But no employer acting alone was able to wipe it out. If one employer tried it, or if one state tried it, the costs of operation rose so high that it was impossible to compete with the employers or states which had failed to act. The moment the Recovery Act was passed, this monstrous thing which neither opinion nor law could reach through years of effort went out in a flash. As a British editorial put it, we did more under a code in one day than they in England had been able to do under the common law in eighty-five years of effort. I use this incident, my friends, not to boast of what has already been done but to point the way to you for even greater cooperative efforts this summer and autumn.

We are not going through another winter like the last. I doubt if ever any people so bravely and cheerfully endured a season half so bitter. We cannot ask America to continue to face such needless hardships. It is time for courageous action, and the Recovery Bill gives us the means to conquer unemployment with exactly the same weapon that we have used to strike down child labor.

The proposition is simply this: If all employers will act together to shorten hours and raise wages we can put people back to work. No employer will suffer, because the relative level of competitive cost will advance by the same amount for all. But if any considerable group should lag or shirk, this great opportunity will pass us by and we will go into another desperate winter. This must not happen.

We have sent out to all employers an agreement which is the result of weeks of consultation. This agreement checks against the voluntary codes of nearly all the large industries which have already been submitted. This blanket agreement carries the unanimous approval of the three boards which I have appointed to advise in this, boards representing the great leaders in labor, in industry, and in social service. The agreement has already brought a flood of approval from every state, and from so wide a cross-section of the common calling of industry that I know it is fair for all. It is a plan— deliberate, reasonable, and just—intended to put into effect at once the most important of the broad principles which are being established, industry by industry, through codes. Naturally, it takes a good deal of organizing and a great many hearings and many months to get these codes perfected and signed, and we cannot wait for all of them to go through. The blanket agreements, however, which I am sending to every employer will start the wheels turning now, and not six months from now.

There are, of course, men, a few of them, who might thwart this great common purpose by seeking selfish advantage. There are adequate penalties in the law, but I am now asking the cooperation that comes from opinion and from
28 conscience. These are the only instruments we shall use in

this great summer offensive against unemployment. But we shall use them to the limit to protect the willing from the laggard and to make the plan succeed.

In war, in the gloom of night attack, soldiers wear a bright badge on their shoulders to be sure that comrades do not fire on comrades. On that principle, those who cooperate in this program must know each other at a glance. That is why we have provided a badge of honor for this purpose, a simple design with a legend, We Do Our Part; and I ask that all those who join with me shall display that badge prominently. It is essential to our purpose.

Already all the great, basic industries have come forward willingly with proposed codes, and in these codes they accept the principles leading to mass reemployment. But, important as is this heartening demonstration, the richest field for results is among the small employers, those whose contribution will give new work for from one to ten people. These smaller employers are indeed a vital part of the backbone of the country, and the success of our plans lies largely in their hands.

Already the telegrams and letters are pouring into the White House—messages from employers who ask that their names be placed on this special roll of honor. They represent great corporations and companies, and partnerships and individuals. I ask that even before the dates set in the agreements which we have sent out, the employers of the country who have not already done so—the big fellows and the little fellows—shall at once write or telegraph to me personally at the White House, expressing their intention of going through with the plan. And it is my purpose to keep posted in the post office of every town, a roll of honor of all those who join with me.

I want to take this occasion to say to the twenty-four governors who are now in conference in San Francisco that nothing thus far has helped in strengthening this great movement more than their resolutions adopted at the very outset of their meeting, giving this plan their instant and unanimous approval, and pledging to support it in their states.

To the men and women whose lives have been darkened by the fact or the fear of unemployment, I am justified in saying a word of encouragement because the codes and the agreements already approved, or about to be passed upon, prove that the plan does raise wages, and that it does put people back to work. You can look on every employer who adopts the plan as one who is doing his part, and those employers deserve well of everyone who works for a living. It will be clear to you, as it is to me, that while the shirking employer may undersell his competitor, the saving he thus makes is made at the expense of his country's welfare.

While we are making this great common effort there should be no discord and dispute. This is no time to cavil or to question the standard set by this universal agreement. It is time for patience and understanding and cooperation. The

30 workers of this country have rights under this law which can-

not be taken from them, and nobody will be permitted to whittle them away but, on the other hand, no aggression is now necessary to attain those rights. The whole country will be united to get them for you. The principle that applies to the employers applies to the workers as well, and I ask you workers to cooperate in the same spirit.

When Andrew Jackson, "Old Hickory," died, someone asked, "Will he go to heaven?" and the answer was, "He will if he wants to." If I am asked whether the American people will pull themselves out of this depression, I answer, "They will if they want to." The essence of the plan is a universal limitation of hours of work per week for any individual by common consent, and a universal payment of wages above the minimum, also by common consent. I cannot guarantee the success of this nationwide plan, but the people of this country can guarantee its success. I have no faith in "cure-alls" but I believe that we can greatly influence economic forces. I have no sympathy with the professional economists who insist that things must run their course and that human agencies can have no influence on economic ills. One reason is that I happen to know that professional economists have changed their definition of economic laws every five or ten years for a very long time. But I do have faith, and retain faith, in the strength of common purpose, and in the strength of unified action taken by the American people.

That is why I am describing to you the simple purposes and the solid foundation upon which our program of recovery is built. That is why I am asking the employers of the nation to sign this common covenant with me—to sign it in the name of patriotism and humanity. That is why I am asking the workers to go along with us in a spirit of understanding and of helpfulness.

OCTOBER 22, 1933

It is three months since I have talked with the people of this country about our national problems; but during this period many things have happened, and I am glad to say that the major part of them have greatly helped the well-being of the average citizens.

Because, in every step which your government is taking we are thinking in terms of the average of you—in the old words, "the greatest good to the greatest number"—we, as reasonable people, cannot expect to bring definite benefits to every person or to every occupation or business, or industry or agriculture. In the same way, no reasonable person can expect that in this short space of time, during which new machinery had to be not only put to work, but first set up, that every locality in every one of the forty-eight states of the country could share equally and simultaneously in the trend to better times.

The whole picture, however—the average of the whole territory from coast to coast, the average of the whole population of 120,000,000 people—shows to any person willing to look, facts and action of which you and I can be proud.

In the early spring of this year there were actually and proportionately more people out of work in this country than in any other nation in the world. Fair estimates showed 12 or 13 millions unemployed last March. Among those there were, of course, several millions who could be classed as normally unemployed—people who worked occasionally when they felt like it, and others who preferred not to work at all. It seems, therefore, fair to say that there were about 10 millions of our citizens who earnestly, and in many cases hungrily, were seeking work and could not get it. Of these, in the short space of a few months, I am convinced that at least 4 millions have been given employment—or, saying it another way, 40 percent of those seeking work have found it.

That does not mean, my friends, that I am satisfied, or that you are satisfied that our work is ended. We have a long way to go but we are on the way.

How are we constructing the edifice of recovery—the temple which, when completed, will no longer be a temple of money changers or of beggars, but rather a temple dedicated to and maintained for a greater social justice, a greater welfare for America—the habitation of a sound economic life? We are building, stone by stone, the columns which will support that habitation. Those columns are many in number, 33 and though for a moment the progress of one column may disturb the progress on the pillar next to it, the work on all of them must proceed without let or hindrance.

We all know that immediate relief for the unemployed was the first essential of such a structure and that is why I speak first of the fact that three hundred thousand young men have been given employment all through this winter in the Civilian Conservation Corps camps in almost every part of the nation.

So, too, we have, as you know, expended greater sums in cooperation with states and localities for work relief and home relief than ever before—sums which during the coming winter cannot be lessened for the very simple reason that though several million people have gone back to work, the necessities of those who have not yet obtained work is more severe than at this time last year.

Then we come to the relief that is being given to those who are in danger of losing their farms or their homes. New machinery had to be set up for farm credit and for home credit in every one of the 3,100 counties of the United States, and every day that passes is saving homes and farms to hundreds of families. I have publicly asked that foreclosures on farms and chattels and on homes be delayed until every mortgagor in the country shall have had full opportunity to take advantage of federal credit. I make the further request which many of you know has already been made through the great federal credit organizations that if there is any family in the United States about to lose its home or about to lose its chattels, that family should telegraph at once either to the Farm Credit Administration or the Home Owners Loan Corporation in Washington requesting their help.

Two other great agencies are in full swing. The Reconstruction Finance Corporation continues to lend large sums to industry and finance with the definite objective of making easy the extending of credit to industry, commerce, and finance.

The program of public works in three months has advanced to this point: Out of a total appropriated for public works of $3,300,000,000, $1,800,000,000 has already been allocated to federal projects of all kinds and literally in every part of the United States and work on these is starting forward. In addition, $300 millions have been allocated to public works to be carried out by states, municipalities, and private organizations, such as those undertaking slum clearance. The balance of the public works money—nearly all of it intended for state or local projects—waits only on the presentation of proper projects by the states and localities themselves. Washington has the money and is waiting for the proper projects to which to allot it.

Another pillar in the making is the Agricultural Adjustment Administration. I have been amazed by the extraordinary degree of cooperation given to the government by the cotton farmers in the South, the wheat farmers of the West, the tobacco farmers of the Southeast, and I am confident that the corn-hog farmers of the Middle West will come through in the same magnificent fashion. The problem we seek to solve had been steadily getting worse for twenty years but during the last six months we have made more rapid progress than any nation has ever made in a like period of time. It is true that in July farm commodity prices had been pushed up higher than they are today, but that push came in part from pure speculation by people who could not tell you the difference between wheat and rye, by people who had never seen cotton growing, by people who did not know that hogs were fed on corn—people who have no real interest in the farmer and his problems.

In spite, however, of the speculative reaction from the speculative advance, it seems to be well established that during the course of the year 1933 the farmers of the United States will receive 33 percent more dollars for what they have produced than they received in the year 1932. Put in another way, they will receive $400 in 1933, where they received $300 the year before. That, remember, is for the average of the country, for I have reports that some sections are not any better off than they were a year ago. This applies among the major products, especially to cattle raising and the dairy industry. We are going after those problems as fast as we can.

I do not hesitate to say, in the simplest, clearest language of which I am capable, that although the prices of many products of the farm have gone up and although many farm families are better off than they were last year, I am not satisfied either with the amount or the extent of the rise, and that it is definitely a part of our policy to increase the rise and to extend it to those products which have as yet felt no benefit. If we cannot do this one way we will do it another. Do it, we will.

Standing beside the pillar of the farm—the AAA—is the pillar of industry—the NRA. Its object is to put industry and business workers into employment and to increase their purchasing power through increased wages.

It has abolished child labor. It had eliminated the sweatshop. It has ended sixty cents a week paid in some mills and eighty cents a week paid in some mines. The measure of the growth of this pillar lies in the total figures of reemployment which I have already given you, and in the fact that reemployment is continuing and not stopping. The secret of NRA is cooperation. That cooperation has been voluntarily given through the signing of the blanket codes and through the signing of specific codes which already include all of the greater industries of the nation.

In the vast majority of cases, in the vast majority of localities—the NRA has been given support in unstinted measure. We know that there are chiselers. At the bottom of every case of criticism and obstruction we have found some selfish interest, some private axe to grind.

Ninety percent of complaints come from misconception. For example, it has been said that NRA has failed to raise the price of wheat and corn and hogs; that NRA has not loaned 37 enough money for local public works. Of course, NRA has nothing whatsoever to do with the price of farm products, nor with public works. It has to do only with industrial organization for economic planning to wipe out unfair practices and to create reemployment. Even in the field of business and industry, NRA does not apply to the rural communities or to towns of under twenty-five hundred population, except insofar as those towns contain factories or chain stores which come under a specific code.

It is also true that among the chiselers to whom I have referred, there are not only the big chiselers but also petty chiselers who seek to make undue profit on untrue statements.

Let me cite to you the example of the salesman in a store in a large eastern city who tried to justify the increase in the price of a cotton shirt from one dollar and a half to two dollars and a half by saying to the customer that it was due to the cotton-processing tax. Actually in that shirt there was about one pound of cotton and the processing tax amounted to four and a quarter cents on that pound of cotton.

At this point it is only fair that I should give credit to the 60 or 70 million people who live in the cities and larger towns of the nation for their understanding and their willingness to go along with the payment of even these small processing taxes, though they know full well that the proportion
of the processing taxes on cotton goods and on food products

paid for by city dwellers goes 100 percent towards increasing the agricultural income of the farm dwellers of the land.

The last pillar of which I speak is that of the money of the country in the banks of the country. There are two simple facts.

First, the federal government is about to spend $1 billion as an immediate loan on the frozen or nonliquid assets of all banks closed since January 1, 1933, giving a liberal appraisal to those assets. This money will be in the hands of the depositors as quickly as it is humanly possible to get it out.

Secondly, the government bank deposit insurance on all accounts up to $2,500 goes into effect on January 1. We are now engaged in seeing to it that on or before that date the banking capital structure will be built up by the government to the point that the banks will be in sound condition when the insurance goes into effect.

Finally, I repeat what I have said on many occasions, that ever since last March the definite policy of the government has been to restore commodity price levels. The object has been the attainment of such a level as will enable agriculture and industry once more to give work to the unemployed. It has been to make possible the payment of public and private debts more nearly at the price level at which they were incurred. It has been gradually to restore a balance in the price structure so that farmers may exchange their products for the products of industry on a fairer exchange basis. It has been and is also the purpose to prevent prices from rising be- 39 yond the point necessary to attain these ends. The permanent welfare and security of every class of our people ultimately depends on our attainment of these purposes.

Obviously, and because hundreds of different kinds of crops and industrial occupations in the huge territory that makes up this nation are involved, we cannot reach the goal in only a few months. We may take one year or two years or three years.

No one who considers the plain facts of our situation believes that commodity prices, especially agricultural prices, are high enough yet.

Some people are putting the cart before the horse. They want a permanent revaluation of the dollar first. It is the government's policy to restore the price level first. I would not know, and no one else could tell, just what the permanent valuation of the dollar will be. To guess at a permanent gold valuation now would certainly require later changes caused by later facts.

When we have restored the price level, we shall seek to establish and maintain a dollar which will not change its purchasing and debt-paying power during the succeeding generation. I said that in my message to the American delegation in London last July. And I say it now once more.

Because of conditions in this country and because of events beyond our control in other parts of the world, it becomes increasingly important to develop and apply the further measures which may be necessary from time to time to control the gold value of our own dollar at home.

Our dollar is now altogether too greatly influenced by the accidents of international trade, by the internal policies of other nations, and by political disturbance in other continents. Therefore the United States must take firmly in its own hands the control of the gold value of our dollar. This is necessary in order to prevent dollar disturbances from swinging us away from our ultimate goal, namely, the continued recovery of our commodity prices.

As a further effective means to this end, I am going to establish a Government market for gold in the United States. Therefore, under the clearly defined authority of existing law, I am authorizing the Reconstruction Finance Corporation to buy gold newly mined in the United States at prices to be determined from time to time after consultation with the secretary of the treasury and the president. Whenever necessary to the end in view, we shall also buy or sell gold in the world market.

My aim in taking this step is to establish and maintain continuous control.

This is a policy and not an expedient.

It is not to be used merely to offset a temporary fall in prices. We are thus continuing to move towards a managed currency.

You will recall the dire predictions made last spring by those who did not agree with our common policies of raising prices by direct means. What actually happened stood out in sharp contrast with those predictions. Government credit is high, prices have risen in part. Doubtless prophets of evil still exist in our midst. But government credit will be maintained and a sound currency will accompany a rise in the American commodity price level.

I have told you tonight the story of our steady but sure work in building our common recovery. In my promises to you both before and after March 4, I made two things plain: First, that I pledged no miracles and, second, that I would do my best.

I thank you for your patience and your faith. Our troubles will not be over tomorrow, but we are on our way and we are headed in the right direction.

World War II

SEPTEMBER 3, 1939

My countrymen and my friends. Tonight my single duty is to speak to the whole of America.

Until four-thirty o'clock this morning I had hoped against hope that some miracle would prevent a devastating war in Europe and bring an end to the invasion of Poland by Germany.

For four long years a succession of actual wars and constant crises have shaken the entire world and have threatened in each case to bring on the gigantic conflict which is today unhappily a fact.

It is right that I should recall to your minds the consistent and at times successful efforts of your government in these crises to throw the full weight of the United States into the cause of peace. In spite of spreading wars I think that we have every right and every reason to maintain as a national policy the fundamental moralities, the teachings of religion, the continuation of efforts to restore peace because some day, though the time may be distant, we can be of even greater help to a crippled humanity.

It is right, too, to point out that the unfortunate events of these recent years have, without question, been based on the use of force or the threat of force. And it seems to me clear, even at the outbreak of this great war, that the influence of America should be consistent in seeking for humanity a final peace which will eliminate, as far as it is possible to do so, the continued use of force between nations.

It is, of course, impossible to predict the future. I have my constant stream of information from American representatives and other sources throughout the world. You, the people of this country, are receiving news through your radios and your newspapers at every hour of the day.

You are, I believe, the most-enlightened and the best-informed people in all the world at this moment. You are subjected to no censorship of news, and I want to add that your government has no information which it withholds or which it has any thought of withholding from you.

At the same time, as I told my press conference on Friday, it is of the highest importance that the press and the radio use the utmost caution to discriminate between actual verified fact on the one hand, and mere rumor on the other.

I can add to that by saying that I hope the people of this country will also discriminate most carefully between news and rumor. Do not believe of necessity everything you hear or read. Check up on it first.

You must master at the outset a simple but unalterable fact in modern relations between nations. When peace has been broken anywhere, the peace of all countries everywhere is in

danger.

It is easy for you and for me to shrug our shoulders and say that conflicts taking place thousands of miles from the continental United States, and, indeed thousands of miles from the whole American hemisphere, do not seriously affect the Americas—and that all the United States has to do is to ignore them and go about its own business. Passionately though we may desire detachment, we are forced to realize that every word that comes through the air, every ship that sails the sea, every battle that is fought, does affect the American future.

Let no man or woman thoughtlessly or falsely talk of America sending its armies to European fields. At this moment there is being prepared a proclamation of American neutrality. This would have been done even if there had been no neutrality statute on the books, for this proclamation is in accordance with international law and in accordance with American policy.

This will be followed by a proclamation required by the existing Neutrality Act. And I trust that in the days to come our neutrality can be made a true neutrality.

It is of the utmost importance that the people of this country, with the best information in the world, think things through. The most dangerous enemies of American peace are those who, without well-rounded information on the whole broad subject of the past, the present, and the future, undertake to speak with assumed authority, to talk in terms of glit- 45 tering generalities, to give to the nation assurances or prophecies which are of little present or future value.

I myself cannot and do not prophesy the course of events abroad—and the reason is that, because I have of necessity such a complete picture of what is going on in every part of the world, that I do not dare to do so. And the other reason is that I think it is honest for me to be honest with the people of the United States.

I cannot prophesy the immediate economic effect of this new war on our nation, but I do say that no American has the moral right to profiteer at the expense either of his fellow citizens or of the men, the women, and the children who are living and dying in the midst of war in Europe.

Some things we do know. Most of us in the United States believe in spiritual values. Most of us, regardless of what church we belong to, believe in the spirit of the New Testament—a great teaching which opposes itself to the use of force, of armed force, of marching armies and falling bombs. The overwhelming masses of our people seek peace—peace at home, and the kind of peace in other lands which will not jeopardize our peace at home.

We have certain ideas and certain ideals of national safety, and we must act to preserve that safety today, and to preserve the safety of our children in future years.

That safety is and will be bound up with the safety of the Western Hemisphere and of the seas adjacent thereto. We

46 seek to keep war from our own firesides by keeping war from

coming to the Americas. For that we have historic precedent that goes back to the days of the administration of President George Washington. It is serious enough and tragic enough to every American family in every state in the Union to live in a world that is torn by wars on other continents. And those wars today affect every American home. It is our national duty to use every effort to keep those wars out of the Americas.

And at this time let me make the simple plea that partisanship and selfishness be adjourned; and that national unity be the thought that underlies all others.

This nation will remain a neutral nation, but I cannot ask that every American remain neutral in thought as well. Even a neutral has a right to take account of facts. Even a neutral cannot be asked to close his mind or close his conscience.

I have said not once, but many times, that I have seen war and that I hate war. I say that again and again.

I hope the United States will keep out of this war. I believe that it will. And I give you assurance and reassurance that every effort of your government will be directed toward that end.

As long as it remains within my power to prevent, there will be no blackout of peace in the United States.

December 29, 1940

My friends, this is not a Fireside Chat on war. It is a talk on national security; because the nub of the whole purpose of your president is to keep you now, and your children later, and your grandchildren much later, out of a last-ditch war for the preservation of American independence and all of the things that American independence means to you and to me and to ours.

Tonight, in the presence of a world crisis, my mind goes back eight years to a night in the midst of a domestic crisis. It was a time when the wheels of American industry were grinding to a full stop, when the whole banking system of our country had ceased to function.

I well remember that while I sat in my study in the White House, preparing to talk with the people of the United States, I had before my eyes the picture of all those Americans with whom I was talking. I saw the workmen in the mills, the mines, the factories; the girl behind the counter; the small shopkeeper; the farmer doing his spring plowing; the widows and the old men wondering about their life's savings. I tried to convey to the great mass of American people what the banking crisis meant to them in their daily lives.

Tonight, I want to do the same thing, with the same people, in this new crisis which faces America.

We met the issue of 1933 with courage and realism.

We face this new crisis—this new threat to the security of our nation—with the same courage and realism.

Never before since Jamestown and Plymouth Rock has our American civilization been in such danger as now.

For on September 27, 1940, this year, by an agreement signed in Berlin, three powerful nations, two in Europe and one in Asia, joined themselves together in the threat that if the United States of America interfered with or blocked the expansion program of these three nations—a program aimed at world control—they would unite in ultimate action against the United States.

The Nazi masters of Germany have made it clear that they intend not only to dominate all life and thought in their own country, but also to enslave the whole of Europe, and then to use the resources of Europe to dominate the rest of the world.

It was only three weeks ago that their leader stated this: "There are two worlds that stand opposed to each other." And then in defiant reply to his opponents, he said this: "Others are correct when they say: With this world we cannot ever reconcile ourselves . . . I can beat any other power in the world." So said the leader of the Nazis.

In other words, the Axis not merely admits, but the Axis *proclaims*, that there can be no ultimate peace between their 49 philosophy, their philosophy of government, and our philosophy of government.

In view of the nature of this undeniable threat, it can be asserted, properly and categorically, that the United States has no right or reason to encourage talk of peace, until the day shall come when there is a clear intention on the part of the aggressor nations to abandon all thought of dominating or conquering the world.

At this moment, the forces of the states that are leagued against all people who live in freedom, are being held away from our shores. The Germans and the Italians are being blocked on the other side of the Atlantic by the British, and by the Greeks, and by thousands of soldiers and sailors who were able to escape from subjugated countries. In Asia, the Japanese are being engaged by the Chinese nation in another great defense.

In the Pacific Ocean is our fleet.

Some of our people like to believe that wars in Europe and in Asia are of no concern to us. But it is a matter of most vital concern to us that European and Asiatic war-makers should not gain control of the oceans which lead to this hemisphere.

One hundred and seventeen years ago the Monroe Doctrine was conceived by our government as a measure of defense in the face of a threat against this hemisphere by an 50 alliance in continental Europe. Thereafter, we stood guard in the Atlantic, with the British as neighbors. There was no treaty. There was no "unwritten agreement."

And yet, there was the feeling, proven correct by history, that we as neighbors could settle any disputes in peaceful fashion. And the fact is that during the whole of this time the Western Hemisphere has remained free from aggression from Europe or from Asia.

Does anyone seriously believe that we need to fear attack anywhere in the Americas while a free Britain remains our most powerful naval neighbor in the Atlantic? And does anyone seriously believe, on the other hand, that we could rest easy if the Axis powers were our neighbors there?

If Great Britain goes down, the Axis powers will control the continents of Europe, Asia, Africa, Australasia, and the high seas—and they will be in a position to bring enormous military and naval resources against this hemisphere. It is no exaggeration to say that all of us, in all the Americas, would be living at the point of a gun—a gun loaded with explosive bullets, economic as well as military.

We should enter upon a new and terrible era in which the whole world, our hemisphere included, would be run by threats of brute force. And to survive in such a world, we would have to convert ourselves permanently into a militaristic power on the basis of war economy.

Some of us like to believe that even if Britain falls, we are still safe, because of the broad expanse of the Atlantic and of the Pacific.

But the width of those oceans is not what it was in the days of clipper ships. At one point between Africa and Brazil the distance is less than it is from Washington to Denver, Colorado—five hours for the latest type of bomber. And at the North end of the Pacific Ocean, America and Asia almost touch each other.

Why even today we have planes that could fly from the British Isles to New England and back again without refueling. And remember that the range of the modern bomber is ever being increased.

During the past week many people in all parts of the nation have told me what they wanted me to say tonight. Almost all of them expressed a courageous desire to hear the plain truth about the gravity of the situation. One telegram, however, expressed the attitude of the small minority who want to see no evil and hear no evil, even though they know in their hearts that evil exists. That telegram begged me not to tell again of the ease with which our American cities could be bombed by any hostile power which had gained bases in this Western Hemisphere. The gist of that telegram was, "Please, Mr. President, don't frighten us by telling us the facts."

Frankly and definitely there is danger ahead—danger against which we must prepare. But we well know that we cannot escape danger, or the fear of danger, by crawling into bed and pulling the covers over our heads.

Some nations of Europe were bound by solemn nonintervention pacts with Germany. Other nations were assured by Germany that they need *never* fear invasion. Nonintervention pact or not, the fact remains that they *were* attacked, overrun, thrown into modern slavery at an hour's notice, or even without any notice at all. As an exiled leader of one of these nations said to me the other day—"The notice was a minus quantity. It was given to my government two hours after German troops had poured into my country in a hundred places."

The fate of these nations tells us what it means to live at the point of a Nazi gun.

The Nazis have justified such actions by various pious frauds. One of these frauds is the claim that they are occupying a nation for the purpose of "restoring order." Another is that they are occupying or controlling a nation on the excuse that they are "protecting it" against the aggression of somebody else.

For example, Germany has said that she was occupying Belgium to save the Belgians from the British. Would she then hesitate to say to any South American country, "We are occupying you to protect you from aggression by the United States"?

Belgium today is being used as an invasion base against Britain, now fighting for its life. And any South American country, in Nazi hands, would always constitute a jumping-off place for German attack on any one of the other republics of this hemisphere.

Analyze for yourselves the future of two other places even nearer to Germany if the Nazis won. Could Ireland hold out? Would Irish freedom be permitted as an amazing pet exception in an unfree world? Or the islands of the Azores, which still fly the flag of Portugal after five centuries? You and I think of Hawaii as an outpost of defense in the Pacific. And yet, the Azores are closer to our shores in the Atlantic than Hawaii is on the other side.

There are those who say that the Axis powers would never have any desire to attack the Western Hemisphere. That is the same dangerous form of wishful thinking which has destroyed the powers of resistance of so many conquered peoples. The plain facts are that the Nazis have proclaimed, time and again, that all other races are their inferiors and therefore subject to their orders. And most important of all, the vast resources and wealth of this American hemisphere constitute the most tempting loot in all of the round world.

Let us no longer blind ourselves to the undeniable fact that the evil forces which have crushed and undermined and corrupted so many others are already within our own gates. Your government knows much about them and every day is ferreting them out.

Their secret emissaries are active in our own and in neighboring countries. They seek to stir up suspicion and dissension to cause internal strife. They try to turn capital against labor, and vice versa. They try to reawaken long-slumbering racial and religious enmities which should have no place in this country. They are active in every group that promotes intolerance. They exploit for their own ends our own natural abhorrence of war. These trouble-breeders have but one purpose. It is to divide our people, to divide them into hostile groups and to destroy our unity and shatter our will to defend ourselves.

There are also American citizens, many of them in high places, who, unwittingly in most cases, are aiding and abetting the work of these agents. I do not charge these American citizens with being foreign agents. But I do charge them with doing exactly the kind of work that the dictators want done in the United States.

These people not only believe that we can save our own skins by shutting our eyes to the fate of other nations. Some of them go much further than that. They say that we can and should become the friends and even the partners of the Axis powers. Some of them even suggest that we should imitate the methods of the dictatorships. But Americans never can and never will do that.

The experience of the past two years has proven beyond doubt that no nation can appease the Nazis. No man can tame a tiger into a kitten by stroking it. There can be no appeasement with ruthlessness. There can be no reasoning with an incendiary bomb. We know now that a nation can have peace with the Nazis only at the price of total surrender.

Even the people of Italy have been forced to become ac- 55

complices of the Nazis; but at this moment they do not know how soon they will be embraced to death by their allies.

The American appeasers ignore the warning to be found in the fate of Austria, Czechoslovakia, Poland, Norway, Belgium, the Netherlands, Denmark, and France. They tell you that the Axis powers are going to win anyway; that all of this bloodshed in the world could be saved; that the United States might just as well throw its influence into the scale of a dictated peace, and get the best out of it that we can.

They call it a "negotiated peace." Nonsense! Is it a negotiated peace if a gang of outlaws surrounds your community and on threat of extermination makes you pay tribute to save your own skins?

For such a dictated peace would be no peace at all. It would be only another armistice, leading to the most gigantic armament race and the most devastating trade wars in all history. And in these contests the Americas would offer the only real resistance to the Axis powers.

With all their vaunted efficiency, with all their parade of pious purpose in this war, there are still in their background the concentration camp and the servants of God in chains.

The history of recent years proves that the shootings and the chains and the concentration camps are not simply the transient tools but the very altars of modern dictatorships. They may talk of a "new order" in the world, but what they have in mind is only a revival of the oldest and the worst tyranny. In that there is no liberty, no religion, no hope.

The proposed "new order" is the very opposite of a United States of Europe or a United States of Asia. It is not a government based upon the consent of the governed. It is not a union of ordinary, self-respecting men and women to protect themselves and their freedom and their dignity from oppression. It is an unholy alliance of power and pelf to dominate and to enslave the human race.

The British people and their allies today are conducting an active war against this unholy alliance. Our own future security is greatly dependent on the outcome of that fight. Our ability to keep out of war is going to be affected by that outcome.

Thinking in terms of today and tomorrow, I make the direct statement to the American people that there is far less chance of the United States getting into war if we do all we can now to support the nations defending themselves against attack by the Axis than if we acquiesce in their defeat, submit tamely to an Axis victory, and wait our turn to be the object of attack in another war later on.

If we are to be completely honest with ourselves, we must admit that there is risk in any course we may take. But I deeply believe that the great majority of our people agree that the course that I advocate involves the least risk now and the greatest hope for world peace in the future.

The people of Europe who are defending themselves do not ask us to do their fighting. They ask us for the implements of war, the planes, the tanks, the guns, the freighters 57 which will enable them to fight for their liberty and for our security. Emphatically we must get these weapons to them, get them to them in sufficient volume and quickly enough, so that we and our children will be saved the agony and suffering of war which others have had to endure.

Let not the defeatists tell us that it is too late. It will never be earlier. Tomorrow will be later than today.

Certain facts are self-evident.

In a military sense Great Britain and the British Empire are today the spearhead of resistance to world conquest. And they are putting up a fight which will live forever in the story of human gallantry.

There is no demand for sending an American Expeditionary Force outside our own borders. There is no intention by any member of your government to send such a force. You can, therefore, nail, nail any talk about sending armies to Europe as deliberate untruth.

Our national policy is not directed toward war. Its sole purpose is to keep war away from our country and away from our people.

Democracy's fight against world conquest is being greatly aided, and must be more greatly aided, by the rearmament of the United States and by sending every ounce and every ton of munitions and supplies that we can possibly spare to help the defenders who are in the front lines. And it is no more

unneutral for us to do that than it is for Sweden, Russia, and other nations near Germany, to send steel and ore and oil and other war materials into Germany every day in the week.

We are planning our own defense with the utmost urgency and in its vast scale we must integrate the war needs of Britain and the other free nations which are resisting aggression.

This is not a matter of sentiment or of controversial personal opinion. It is a matter of realistic, practical military policy, based on the advice of our military experts who are in close touch with existing warfare. These military and naval experts and the members of the Congress and the administration have a single-minded purpose—the defense of the United States.

This nation is making a great effort to produce everything that is necessary in this emergency—and with all possible speed. And this great effort requires great sacrifice.

I would ask no one to defend a democracy which in turn would not defend everyone in the nation against want and privation. The strength of this nation shall not be diluted by the failure of the government to protect the economic well-being of its citizens.

If our capacity to produce is limited by machines, it must ever be remembered that these machines are operated by the skill and the stamina of the worker. As the government is determined to protect the rights of the workers, so the nation has a right to expect that the men who man the machines will discharge their full responsibilities to the urgent needs of defense.

The worker possesses the same human dignity and is entitled to the same security of position as the engineer or the manager or the owner. For the workers provide the human power that turns out the destroyers, and the planes and the tanks.

The nation expects our defense industries to continue operation without interruption by strikes or lockouts. It expects and insists that management and workers will reconcile their differences by voluntary or legal means, to continue to produce the supplies that are so sorely needed.

And on the economic side of our great defense program, we are, as you know, bending every effort to maintain stability of prices and with that the stability of the cost of living.

Nine days ago I announced the setting up of a more effective organization to direct our gigantic efforts to increase the production of munitions. The appropriation of vast sums of money and a well-coordinated executive direction of our defense efforts are not in themselves enough. Guns, planes, ships, and many other things have to be built in the factories and the arsenals of America. They have to be produced by workers and managers and engineers with the aid of machines which in turn have to be built by hundreds of thousands of workers throughout the land.

In this great work there has been splendid cooperation between the government and industry and labor; and I am very thankful.

60   American industrial genius, unmatched throughout all the

world in the solution of production problems, has been called upon to bring its resources and its talents into action. Manufacturers of watches, of farm implements, of linotypes and cash registers and automobiles and sewing machines and lawn mowers and locomotives are now making fuses and bomb packing crates and telescope mounts and shells and pistols and tanks.

But all of our present efforts are not enough. We must have more ships, more guns, more planes—more of everything. And this can be accomplished only if we discard the notion of "business as usual." This job cannot be done merely by superimposing on the existing productive facilities the added requirements of the nation for defense.

Our defense efforts must not be blocked by those who fear the future consequences of surplus plant capacity. The possible consequences of failure of our defense efforts now are much more to be feared.

And after the present needs of our defense are past, a proper handling of the country's peacetime needs will require all of the new productive capacity—if not still more.

No pessimistic policy about the future of America shall delay the immediate expansion of those industries essential to defense. We need them.

I want to make it clear that it is the purpose of the nation to build now with all possible speed every machine, every arsenal, every factory that we need to manufacture our defense 61 material. We have the men, the skill, the wealth, and above all, the will.

I am confident that if and when production of consumer or luxury goods in certain industries requires the use of machines and raw materials that are essential for defense purposes, then such production must yield, and will gladly yield, to our primary and compelling purpose.

So I appeal to the owners of plants—to the managers, to the workers, to our own government employees—to put every ounce of effort into producing these munitions swiftly and without stint. With this appeal I give you the pledge that all of us who are officers of your government will devote ourselves to the same wholehearted extent to the great task that lies ahead.

As planes and ships and guns and shells are produced, your government, with its defense experts, can then determine how best to use them to defend this hemisphere. The decision as to how much shall be sent abroad and how much shall remain at home must be made on the basis of our overall military necessities.

We must be the great arsenal of democracy. For us this is an emergency as serious as war itself. We must apply ourselves to our task with the same resolution, the same sense of urgency, the same spirit of patriotism and sacrifice as we would show were we at war.

We have furnished the British great material support and we will furnish far more in the future.

There will be no bottlenecks in our determination to aid Great Britain. No dictator, no combination of dictators, will weaken that determination by threats of how they will construe that determination.

The British have received invaluable military support from the heroic Greek army, and from the forces of all the governments in exile. Their strength is growing. It is the strength of men and women who value their freedom more highly than they value their lives.

I believe that the Axis powers are not going to win this war. I base that belief on the latest and best of information.

We have no excuse for defeatism. We have every good reason for hope—hope for peace, yes, and hope for the defense of our civilization and for the building of a better civilization in the future.

I have the profound conviction that the American people are now determined to put forth a mightier effort than they have ever yet made to increase our production of all the implements of defense, to meet the threat to our democratic faith.

As president of the United States I call for that national effort. I call for it in the name of this nation which we love and honor and which we are privileged and proud to serve. I call upon our people with absolute confidence that our common cause will greatly succeed.

DECEMBER 9, 1941

My fellow Americans. The sudden criminal attacks perpetrated by the Japanese in the Pacific provide the climax of a decade of international immorality.

Powerful and resourceful gangsters have banded together to make war upon the whole human race. Their challenge has now been flung at the United States of America. The Japanese have treacherously violated the long-standing peace between us. Many American soldiers and sailors have been killed by enemy action. American ships have been sunk; American airplanes have been destroyed.

The Congress and the people of the United States have accepted that challenge.

Together with other free peoples, we are now fighting to maintain our right to live among our world neighbors in freedom, in common decency, without fear of assault.

I have prepared the full record of our past relations with Japan, and it will be submitted to the Congress. It begins with the visit of Commodore Perry to Japan eighty-eight years ago. It ends with the visit of two Japanese emissaries 64 to the secretary of state last Sunday, an hour after Japanese forces had loosed their bombs and machine guns against our flag, our forces, and our citizens.

I can say with utmost confidence that no Americans, today or a thousand years hence, need feel anything but pride in our patience and in our efforts through all the years toward achieving a peace in the Pacific which would be fair and honorable to every nation, large or small. And no honest person, today or a thousand years hence, will be able to suppress a sense of indignation and horror at the treachery committed by the military dictators of Japan, under the very shadow of the flag of peace borne by their special envoys in our midst.

The course that Japan has followed for the past ten years in Asia has paralleled the course of Hitler and Mussolini in Europe and in Africa. Today, it has become far more than a parallel. It is collaboration, actual collaboration, so well calculated that all the continents of the world, and all the oceans, are now considered by the Axis strategists as one gigantic battlefield.

In 1931, ten years ago, Japan invaded Manchukuo—without warning.

In 1935, Italy invaded Ethiopia—without warning.

In 1938, Hitler occupied Austria—without warning.

In 1939, Hitler invaded Czechoslovakia—without warning.

Later in '39, Hitler invaded Poland—without warning.

In 1940, Hitler invaded Norway, Denmark, the Netherlands, Belgium, and Luxembourg—without warning.

In 1940, Italy attacked France and later Greece—without warning.

And this year, in 1941, the Axis powers attacked Yugoslavia and Greece and they dominated the Balkans—without warning.

In 1941, also, Hitler invaded Russia—without warning.

And now Japan has attacked Malaya and Thailand—and the United States—without warning.

It is all of one pattern.

We are now in this war. We are all in it—all the way. Every single man, woman, and child is a partner in the most tremendous undertaking of our American history. We must share together the bad news and the good news, the defeats and the victories—the changing fortunes of war.

So far, the news has been all bad. We have suffered a serious setback in Hawaii. Our forces in the Philippines, which include the brave people of that commonwealth, are taking punishment, but are defending themselves vigorously. The reports from Guam and Wake and Midway islands are still confused, but we must be prepared for the announcements that all these three outposts have been seized.

The casualty lists of these first few days will undoubtedly be large. I deeply feel the anxiety of all of the families of the men in our armed forces and the relatives of people in cities which have been bombed. I can only give them my solemn promise that they will get news just as quickly as possible.

This government will put its trust in the stamina of the

American people, and will give the facts to the public just as soon as two conditions have been fulfilled: first, that the information has been definitely and officially confirmed; and, second, that the release of the information at the time it is received will not prove valuable to the enemy directly or indirectly.

Most earnestly I urge my countrymen to reject all rumors. These ugly little hints of complete disaster fly thick and fast in wartime. They have to be examined and appraised.

As an example, I can tell you frankly that until further surveys are made, I have not sufficient information to state the exact damage which has been done to our naval vessels at Pearl Harbor. Admittedly the damage is serious. But no one can say how serious, until we know how much of this damage can be repaired and how quickly the necessary repairs can be made.

I cite as another example a statement made on Sunday night that a Japanese carrier had been located and sunk off the canal zone. And when you hear statements that are attributed to what they call "an authoritative source," you can be reasonably sure from now on that under these war circumstances the "authoritative source" is not any person in authority.

Many rumors and reports which we now hear originate of course with enemy sources. For instance, today the Japanese are claiming that as a result of their one action against Hawaii they have gained naval supremacy in the Pacific. This is 67 an old trick of propaganda which has been used innumerable times by the Nazis. The purposes of such fantastic claims are, of course, to spread fear and confusion among us, and to goad us into revealing military information which our enemies are desperately anxious to obtain.

Our government will not be caught in this obvious trap—and neither will the people of the United States.

It must be remembered by each and every one of us that our free and rapid communication these days must be greatly restricted in wartime. It is not possible to receive full and speedy and accurate reports from distant areas of combat. This is particularly true where naval operations are concerned. For in these days of the marvels of the radio it's often impossible for the commanders of various units to report their activities by radio at all, for the very simple reason that this information would become available to the enemy, and would disclose their position and their plan of defense or attack.

Of necessity there will be delays in officially confirming or denying reports of operations, but we will not hide facts from the country if we know the facts and if the enemy will not be aided by their disclosure.

To all newspapers and radio stations—all those who reach the eyes and ears of the American people—I say this: You have a most grave responsibility to the nation now and for the duration of this war.

If you feel that your government is not disclosing enough 68 of the truth, you have every right to say so. But—in the absence of all the facts, as revealed by official sources—you have no right in the ethics of patriotism to deal out unconfirmed reports in such a way as to make people believe that they are gospel truth.

Every citizen, in every walk of life, shares this same responsibility. The lives of our soldiers and sailors—the whole future of this nation—depend upon the manner in which each and every one of us fulfills his obligation to our country.

Now a word about the recent past—and the future. A year and a half has elapsed since the fall of France, when the whole world first realized the mechanized might which the Axis nations had been building up for so many years. America has used that year and a half to great advantage. Knowing that the attack might reach us in all too short a time, we immediately began greatly to increase our industrial strength and our capacity to meet the demands of modern warfare.

Precious months were gained by sending vast quantities of our war material to the nations of the world still able to resist Axis aggression. Our policy rested on the fundamental truth that the defense of any country resisting Hitler or Japan was in the long run the defense of our own country. That policy has been justified. It has given us time, invaluable time, to build our American assembly lines of production.

Assembly lines are now in operation. Others are being rushed to completion. A steady stream of tanks and planes, of guns and ships and shells and equipment—that is what these eighteen months have given us.

69

But it is all only a beginning of what still has to be done. We must be set to face a long war against crafty and powerful bandits. The attack at Pearl Harbor can be repeated at any one of many points, points in both oceans and along both our coast lines and against all the rest of the hemisphere.

It will not only be a long war, it will be a hard war. That is the basis on which we now lay all our plans. That is the yardstick by which we measure what we shall need and demand; money, materials, doubled and quadrupled production—ever-increasing. The production must be not only for our own Army and Navy and Air Forces. It must reinforce the other armies and navies and air forces fighting the Nazis and the warlords of Japan throughout the Americas and throughout the world.

I have been working today on the subject of production. Your government has decided on two broad policies.

The first is to speed up all existing production by working on a seven-day-week basis in every war industry, including the production of essential raw materials.

The second policy, now being put into form, is to rush additions to the capacity of production by building more new plants, by adding to old plants, and by using the many smaller plants for war needs.

Over the hard road of the past months, we have at times met obstacles and difficulties, divisions and disputes, indifference and callousness. That is now all past—and, I am sure, forgotten.

70

The fact is that the country now has an organization in Washington built around men and women who are recognized experts in their own fields. I think the country knows that the people who are actually responsible in each and every one of these many fields are pulling together with a teamwork that has never before been excelled.

On the road ahead there lies hard work—grueling work—day and night, every hour and every minute.

I was about to add that ahead there lies sacrifice for all of us.

But it is not correct to use that word. The United States does not consider it a sacrifice to do all one can, to give one's best to our nation, when the nation is fighting for its existence and its future life.

It is not a sacrifice for any man, old or young, to be in the Army or the Navy of the United States. Rather it is a privilege.

It is not a sacrifice for the industrialist or the wage earner, the farmer or the shopkeeper, the trainman or the doctor, to pay more taxes, to buy more bonds, to forego extra profits, to work longer or harder at the task for which he is best fitted. Rather it is a privilege.

It is not a sacrifice to do without many things to which we are accustomed if the national defense calls for doing without it.

A review this morning leads me to the conclusion that at present we shall not have to curtail the normal use of articles of food. There is enough food today for all of us and enough left over to send to those who are fighting on the same side with us.

But there will be a clear and definite shortage of metals for many kinds of civilian use, for the very good reason that in our increased program we shall need for war purposes more than half of that portion of the principal metals which during the past year have gone into articles for civilian use. Yes, we shall have to give up many things entirely.

And I am sure that the people in every part of the nation are prepared in their individual living to win this war. I am sure that they will cheerfully help to pay a large part of its financial cost while it goes on. I am sure they will cheerfully give up those material things that they are asked to give up.

And I am sure that they will retain all those great spiritual things without which we cannot win through.

I repeat that the United States can accept no result save victory, final, complete. Not only must the shame of Japanese treachery be wiped out, but the sources of international brutality, wherever they exist, must be absolutely and finally broken.

In my message to the Congress yesterday I said that we "will make very certain that this form of treachery shall never endanger us again." In order to achieve that certainty, we must begin the great task that is before us by abandoning once and for all the illusion that we can ever again isolate
72 ourselves from the rest of humanity.

In these past few years—and, most violently, in the past three days—we have learned a terrible lesson.

It is our obligation to our dead—it is our sacred obligation to their children and to our children—that we must never forget what we have learned.

And what we have learned is this:

There is no such thing as security for any nation—or any individual—in a world ruled by the principles of gangsterism.

There is no such thing as impregnable defense against powerful aggressors who sneak up in the dark and strike without warning.

We have learned that our ocean-girt hemisphere is not immune from severe attack—that we cannot measure our safety in terms of miles on any map anymore.

We may acknowledge that our enemies have performed a brilliant feat of deception, perfectly timed and executed with great skill. It was a thoroughly dishonorable deed, but we must face the fact that modern warfare as conducted in the Nazi manner is a dirty business. We don't like it—we didn't want to get in it—but we are in it and we're going to fight it with everything we've got.

I do not think any American has any doubt of our ability to administer proper punishment to the perpetrators of these crimes.

Your government knows that for weeks Germany has been telling Japan that if Japan did not attack the United States, Japan would not share in dividing the spoils with Germany when peace came. She was promised by Germany that if she came in she would receive the complete and perpetual control of the whole of the Pacific area—and that means not only the Far East, but also all of the islands in the Pacific, and also a stranglehold on the west coast of North and Central and South America.

We know also that Germany and Japan are conducting their military and naval operations in accordance with a joint plan. That plan considers all peoples and nations which are not helping the Axis powers as common enemies of each and every one of the Axis powers.

That is their simple and obvious grand strategy. The American people must realize that it can be matched only with similar grand strategy. We must realize for example that Japanese successes against the United States in the Pacific are helpful to German operations in Libya; that any German success against the Caucasus is inevitably an assistance to Japan in her operations against the Dutch East Indies; that a German attack against Algiers or Morocco opens the way to a German attack against South America and the Canal.

On the other side of the picture, we must learn also to know that guerilla warfare against the Germans in, let us say, Serbia or Norway helps us; that a successful Russian offensive against the Germans helps us; and that British successes on land or sea in any part of the world strengthen our hands.

Remember always that Germany and Italy, regardless of
74 any formal declaration of war, consider themselves at war

with the United States at this moment just as much as they consider themselves at war with Britain or Russia. And Germany puts all the other republics of the Americas into the same category of enemies. The people of our sister republics of this hemisphere can be honored by that fact.

The true goal we seek is far above and beyond the ugly field of battle. When we resort to force, as now we must, we are determined that this force shall be directed toward ultimate good as well as against immediate evil. We Americans are not destroyers—we are builders.

We are now in the midst of a war, not for conquest, not for vengeance, but for a world in which this nation, and all that this nation represents, will be safe for our children. We expect to eliminate the danger from Japan, but it would serve us ill if we accomplished that and found that the rest of the world was dominated by Hitler and Mussolini.

So, we are going to win the war and we are going to win the peace that follows.

And in these difficult hours of this day—through the dark days that may be yet to come—we will know that the vast majority of the members of the human race are on our side. Many of them are fighting with us. All of them are praying for us. For in representing our cause, we represent theirs as well—our hope and their hope for liberty under God.

JANUARY 11, 1944

Ladies and gentlemen. Today I sent my annual Message to the Congress, as required by the Constitution. It has been my custom to deliver these annual Messages in person, and they have been broadcast to the nation. I intended to follow this same custom this year.

But, like a great many other people, I have had the flu, and although I am practically recovered, my doctor simply would not let me leave the White House to go up to the Capitol.

Only a few of the newspapers of the United States can print the Message in full, and I am anxious that the American people be given an opportunity to hear what I have recommended to the Congress for this very fateful year in our history—and the reasons for these recommendations. Here is what I said:

This nation in the past two years has become an active partner in the world's greatest war against human slavery.

We have joined with like-minded people in order to defend ourselves in a world that has been gravely threatened with gangster rule.

But I do not think that any of us Americans can be content with mere survival. Sacrifices that we and our allies are making impose upon all of us a sacred obligation to see to it that out of this war we and our children will gain something better than mere survival.

We are united in determination that this war shall not be followed by another interim which leads to new disaster— that we shall not repeat the tragic errors of ostrich isolationism.

When Mr. Hull went to Moscow in October, when I went to Cairo and Teheran in November, we knew that we were in agreement with our allies in our common determination to fight and win this war. There were many vital questions concerning the future peace, and they were discussed in an atmosphere of complete candor and harmony.

In the last war such discussions, such meetings, did not even begin until the shooting had stopped and the delegates began to assemble at the peace table. There had been no previous opportunities for man-to-man discussions which lead to meetings of minds and the result was a peace which was not a peace.

And right here I want to address a word or two to some suspicious souls who are fearful that Mr. Hull or I have made "commitments" for the future which might pledge this nation to secret treaties or to enacting the role of a world Santa Claus.

Of course we made commitments. For instance we most certainly committed ourselves to very large and very specific military plans which require the use of all Allied forces to bring about the defeat of our enemies at the earliest possible time.

But there were no secret treaties or political or financial commitments.

The one supreme objective for the future, which we discussed for each nation individually, and for all the United Nations, can be summed up in one word: security.

And that means not only physical security which provides safety from attacks by aggressors. It means also economic security, social security, moral security—in a family of nations.

In the plain down-to-earth talks that I had with the Generalissimo and Marshal Stalin and Prime Minister Churchill, it was abundantly clear that they are all most deeply interested in the resumption of peaceful progress by their own peoples—progress toward a better life.

All our allies have learned by bitter experience that real development will not be possible if they are to be diverted from their purpose by repeated wars—or even threats of wars.

The best interests of each nation, large and small, demand that all freedom-loving nations shall join together in a just and durable system of peace. In the present world situation, evidenced by the actions of Germany and Italy and Japan, unquestioned military control over disturbers of the peace is as necessary among nations as it is among citizens in any
community. And an equally basic essential to peace, perma-

nent peace, is a decent standard of living for all individual men and women and children in all nations. Freedom from fear is eternally linked with freedom from want.

There are, of course, people who burrow, burrow through the nation like unseeing moles, and attempt to spread the suspicion that if other nations are encouraged to raise their standards of living, our own American standard of living must of necessity be depressed.

The fact is the very contrary. It has been shown time and again that if the standard of living of any country goes up, so does its purchasing power—and that such a rise encourages a better standard of living in neighboring countries with whom it trades. That is just plain common sense—and is the kind of plain common sense that provided the basis of our discussions at Moscow and Cairo and Teheran.

Returning from my journeyings, I must confess to a sense of being "let down" when I found many evidences of faulty perspectives here in Washington. The faulty perspective consists in overemphasizing lesser problems and thereby underemphasizing the first and greatest problem.

The overwhelming majority of our people have met the demands of this war with magnificent courage and a great deal of understanding. They have accepted inconveniences; they have accepted hardships; they have accepted tragic sacrifices.

However, while the majority goes on about its great work without complaint, we all know that a noisy minority main- 79 tains an uproar, an uproar of demands for special favors for special groups. There are pests who swarm through the lobbies of the Congress and the cocktail bars of Washington, representing these special groups, as opposed to the basic interest of the nation as a whole. They have come to look upon the war primarily as a chance to make profits for themselves at the expense of their neighbors—profits in money or profits in terms of political or social preferment.

Such selfish agitation can be and is highly dangerous in wartime. It creates confusion. It damages morale. It hampers our national effort, it prolongs the war.

In this war, we have been compelled to learn how interdependent upon each other are all groups and sections of the whole population of America.

Increased food costs, for example, will bring new demands for wage increases from all war workers, which will in turn raise all prices of all things, including those things which the farmers themselves have to buy. Increased wages or prices will each in turn produce the same results. They all have a particularly disastrous result on all fixed-income groups.

And I hope you will remember that all of us in this government including myself represent the fixed-income group just as much as we represent business owners or workers or farmers. This group of fixed-income people includes teachers and clergy and policemen and firemen and widows and minors who are on fixed incomes, wives and dependents of our soldiers and sailors, and old-age pensioners. They and their families add up to more than a quarter of our 130 million people. They have few or no high-pressure representatives at the Capitol. And in a period of gross inflation they would be the worst sufferers. Let us give them an occasional thought.

If ever there was a time to subordinate individual or group selfishness to the national good, that time is now. Disunity at home—bickerings, self-seeking partisanship, stoppages of work, inflation, business as usual, politics as usual, luxury as usual, and sometimes a failure to tell the whole truth, these are the influences which can undermine the morale of the brave men ready to die at the front for us here.

Those who are doing most of the complaining, I do not think that they are deliberately striving to sabotage the national war effort. They are laboring under the delusion that the time is past when we must make prodigious sacrifices— that the war is already won and we can begin to slacken off. But the dangerous folly of that point of view can be measured by the distance that separates our troops from their ultimate objectives in Berlin and Tokyo—and by the sum of all the perils that lie along the way.

Overconfidence and complacency are among our deadliest of all enemies.

That attitude on the part of anyone—government or management or labor—can lengthen this war. It can kill American boys.

Let us remember the lessons of 1918. In the summer of

that year the tide turned in favor of the Allies. But this government did not relax, nor did the American people. In fact, our national effort was stepped up. In August 1918, the draft age limits were broadened from twenty-one to thirty-one, all the way to eighteen to forty-five. The president called for "force to the utmost," and his call was heeded. And in November, only three months later, Germany surrendered.

That is the way to fight and win a war—all out—and not with half an eye on the battlefronts abroad and the other eye and a half on personal, selfish, or political interests here at home.

Therefore, in order to concentrate all of our energies, all of our resources on winning this war, and to maintain a fair and stable economy at home, I recommend that the Congress adopt:

First, a realistic and simplified tax law—which will tax all unreasonable profits, both individual and corporate, and reduce the ultimate cost of the war to our sons and our daughters. The tax bill now under consideration by the Congress does not begin to meet this test.

Secondly, a continuation of the law for the renegotiation of war contracts—which will prevent exorbitant profits and assure fair prices to the government. For two long years I have pleaded with the Congress to take undue profits out of war.

Third, a cost of food law—which will enable the government to place a reasonable floor under the prices the farmer may expect for his production; and to place a ceiling on the prices a consumer will have to pay for the necessary food he buys. This should apply, as I have intimated, to necessities only and this will require public finds to carry it out. It will cost in appropriations about 1 percent of the present annual cost of the war.

Fourth, an early reenactment of the stabilization statute of October 1942. This expires this year, June 30, 1944, and if it is not extended well in advance, the country might just as well expect price chaos by summertime.

We cannot have stabilization by wishful thinking. We must take positive action to maintain the integrity of the American dollar.

And fifth, a national service law—which, for the duration of the war, will prevent strikes, and, with certain appropriate exceptions, will make available for war production or for any other essential services every able-bodied adult in this whole nation.

These five measures together form a just and equitable whole. I would not recommend a national service law unless the other laws were passed to keep down the cost of living, to share equitably the burdens of taxation, to hold the stabilization line, and to prevent undue profits.

The federal government already has the basic power to draft capital and property of all kinds for war purposes on the basis of just compensation.

And as you know, I have for three years hesitated to recommend a national service act. Today, however, with all the experience we have behind us and with us, I am convinced of its necessity. Although I believe that we and our allies can win the war without such a measure, I am certain that nothing less than total mobilization of all our resources of manpower and capital will guarantee an earlier victory, and reduce the toll of suffering and sorrow and blood. As some of my advisers wrote me the other day:

> When the very life of a nation is in peril the responsibility for service is common to all men and women. In such a time there can be no discrimination between the men and women who are assigned by the government to its defense at the battlefront and the men and women assigned to producing the vital materials that are essential to successful military operations. A prompt enactment of a National Service Law would be merely an expression of the universality of this American responsibility.

I believe the country will agree that these statements are the solemn truth.

National service is the most democratic way to wage a war. Like Selective Service for the armed forces, it rests on the obligation of each citizen to serve his nation, to his utmost, where he is best qualified.

It does not mean reduction in wages. It does not mean loss of retirement and seniority rights and benefits. It does not mean that any substantial numbers of war workers will be
84 disturbed in their present jobs. Let this fact be wholly clear.

But there are millions of American men and women who are not in this war at all. It is not because they do not want to be in it. But they want to know where they can best do their share. National service provides that direction.

I know that all civilian war workers will be glad to be able to say many years hence to their grandchildren: "Yes, I, too, was in service in the great war. I was on duty in an airplane factory, and I helped to make hundreds of fighting planes. The government told me that in doing that I was performing my most useful work in the service of my country."

It is argued that we have passed the stage in the war where national service is necessary. But our soldiers and sailors know that this is not true. We are going forward on a long, rough road—and, in all journeys, the last miles are the hardest. And it is for that final effort—for the total defeat of our enemies—that we must mobilize our total resources. The national war program calls for the employment of more people in 1944 than in 1943.

And it is my conviction that the American people will welcome this win-the-war measure which is based on the eternally just principle of "fair for one, fair for all."

It will give our people at home the assurance that they are standing four-square behind our soldiers and sailors. And it will give our enemies demoralizing assurance that we mean business—that we, 130 million Americans, are on the march to Rome and Berlin and Tokyo.

I hope that the Congress will recognize that, although this 85 is a political year, national service is an issue which transcends politics. Great power must be used for great purposes.

And as to the machinery for this measure, the Congress itself should determine its nature—as long as it is wholly nonpartisan in its make-up.

Several alleged reasons have prevented the enactment of legislation which would preserve for our soldiers and sailors and marines the fundamental prerogative of citizenship, in other words, the right to vote. No amount of legalistic argument can becloud this issue in the eyes of these 10 million American citizens. Surely the signers of the Constitution did not intend a document which, even in wartime, would be construed to take away the franchise of any of those who are fighting to preserve the Constitution itself.

Our soldiers and sailors and marines know that the overwhelming majority of them will be deprived of the opportunity to vote, if the voting machinery is left exclusively to the states under existing state laws—and that there is no likelihood of these laws being changed in time to enable them to vote at the next election. The Army and Navy have reported that it will be impossible effectively to administer forty-eight different soldier-voting laws. It is the duty of the Congress to remove this unjustifiable discrimination against the men and women in our armed forces—and to do it just as quickly as possible.

It is our duty now to begin to lay the plans and determine
the strategy for more than the winning of the war, it is time

to begin the plans and determine the strategy for winning a lasting peace and the establishment of an American standard of living higher than ever known before.

This republic had its beginning, and grew to its present strength, under the protection of certain inalienable political rights—among them the right of free speech, free press, free worship, trial by jury, freedom from unreasonable searches and seizures. They were our rights to life and liberty.

We have come to a clearer realization of the fact, however, that true individual freedom cannot exist without economic security and independence. "Necessitous men are not free men." People who are hungry, people who are out of a job are the stuff of which dictatorships are made.

In our day these economic truths have become accepted as self-evident. We have accepted, so to speak, a second Bill of Rights under which a new basis of security and prosperity can be established for all—regardless of station or race or creed.

Among these are:

> the right to a useful and remunerative job in the industries or shops or farms or mines of the nation;
> the right to earn enough to provide adequate food and clothing and recreation;
> the right of farmers to raise and sell their products at a return which will give them and their families a decent living;
> the right of every businessman, large and small, to trade in an

atmosphere of freedom from unfair competition and domination by monopolies at home or abroad;

the right of every family to a decent home;

the right to adequate medical care and the opportunity to achieve and enjoy good health;

the right to adequate protection from the economic fears of old age and sickness and accident and unemployment; and, finally,

the right to a good education.

All of these rights spell security. And after this war is won, we must be prepared to move forward in the implementation of these rights, to new goals of human happiness and well-being.

America's own rightful place in the world depends in large part upon how fully these and similar rights have been carried into practice for all our citizens. For unless there is security here at home there cannot be lasting peace in the world.

One of the great American industrialists of our day—a man who has rendered yeoman service to his country in this crisis—recently emphasized the grave dangers of "rightist reaction" in this nation. All clear-thinking businessmen share that concern. Indeed, if such reaction should develop—if history were to repeat itself and we were to return to the so-called normalcy of the 1920s—then it is certain that even though we shall have conquered our enemies on the battlefields abroad, we shall have yielded to the spirit of Fascism here at home.

I ask the Congress to explore the means for implementing this economic bill of rights—for it is definitely the responsibility of the Congress so to do, and the country knows it. Many of these problems are already before committees of the Congress in the form of proposed legislation. I shall from time to time communicate with the Congress with respect to these and further proposals. In the event that no adequate program of progress is evolved, I am certain that the nation will be conscious of the fact.

Our fighting men abroad—and their families at home— expect such a program and have the right to insist on it. It is to their demands that this government should pay heed rather than to the whining demands of selfish pressure groups who seek to feather their nests while young Americans are dying.

I have often said that there are no two fronts for America in this war. There is only one front. There is one line of unity which extends from the hearts of the people at home to the men of our attacking forces in our farthest outposts. When we speak of our total effort, we speak of the factory and the field and the mine as well as of the battlefield—we speak of the soldier and the civilian, the citizen and his government.

Each and every one of us has a solemn obligation under God to serve this nation in its most critical hour—to keep this nation great—to make this nation greater in a better world.

FOR THE BEST IN PAPERBACKS, LOOK FOR THE

In every corner of the world, on every subject under the sun, Penguin represents quality and variety—the very best in publishing today.

For complete information about books available from Penguin—including Puffins, Penguin Classics, and Arkana—and how to order them, write to us at the appropriate address below. Please note that for copyright reasons the selection of books varies from country to country.